Wild and Tame

Wild and Tame

Poems by

Nancy Jo Allen

© 2023 Nancy Jo Allen. All rights reserved.
This material may not be reproduced in any form, published,
reprinted, recorded, performed, broadcast,
rewritten or redistributed without
the explicit permission of Nancy Jo Allen.
All such actions are strictly prohibited by law.

Front cover image by unknown photographer
Back cover image by Jeffery Clayton
Cover design by Shay Culligan

ISBN: 978-1-63980-406-1

Kelsay Books
502 South 1040 East, A-119
American Fork, Utah 84003
Kelsaybooks.com

© 2023 Nancy Jo Allen. All rights reserved.
This material may not be reproduced in any form, published,
reprinted, recorded, performed, broadcast,
rewritten or redistributed without
the explicit permission of Nancy Jo Allen.
All such actions are strictly prohibited by law.

Front cover image by unknown photographer
Back cover image by Jeffery Clayton
Cover design by Shay Culligan

ISBN: 978-1-63980-406-1

Kelsay Books
502 South 1040 East, A-119
American Fork, Utah 84003
Kelsaybooks.com

Wild and Tame

Poems by

Nancy Jo Allen

Acknowledgments

The author is grateful to the editors of the following journals where these poems first appeared, some in earlier versions. A special acknowledgment for Marta Ferguson, whose ability to find the book in the pile of letters and stanzas shapes these pages.

Ancient Paths: "Sepulchers"

Boundless Anthology: "Cafuné"

Common Ground: "Medusa of the Deep"

Dime Show Review: "Fate"

Down in the Dirt: "Palimpsest"

I-70 Review: "Hummingbirds"

Interpretations: "Cleaning Fish," "Form and Function," "Winging Home," "Shoebox," "Roadkill," "Wallpaper and Cranes"

MasticadoresUSA: "Battlefields to Greenhouses"

Star 82: "Beneficiaries," "Brackish-water Crab," "Friday Afternoons"

Well Versed: "Fractured Since 1848," "Mutual Trust" (originally titled "Harvey"), "Mystery," "Red Poppies," "Otis," "Passage"

Contents

Forest, Garden, Sea

Dark Forests and Mountain Tops	15
The Hawk: Part One	17
The Hawk: Part Two	19
Winging Home	20
The Forest	21
Northwestern Wilds	22
Mutual Trust	23
Otis	24
White Hair and Red Yarn	25
I Walk the Dog	26
This Natural World	27
Battlefields to Greenhouses	28
Splitting Hares	31
Protecting the Dray	32
Red Poppies	34
Mystery	36
In the Wings	37
Hummingbirds Hover Out My Office Window	39
Fate	40
Shoebox	41
Roadkill	42
Composting Irises	43
Caterpillar	44
Beneath Missouri's Bootheel	45
Beneficiaries	47
Aesop's Fable: Reward	48
Another Day	49
Medusa of the Deep	50
Waddles	51
Onsra	52
Accidental Fishing	54
Brackish-water Crab	55
Bullhead	56

An Artistic Interlude

An Orchestra	59
Period Piece	60
Journey	61
River Bank, 1910	62
Form and Function	63
Fractured Since 1848	64
Anita, Christine and E. Jean	65

Beloveds and Others

Cafuné	68
Gardening	69
Cleaning Fish	70
Strategies	71
Friday Afternoons	72
Before Sunrise	73
It's the Feast of St. Nicholas Again	74
The Kiss	75
Rearview Mirror	76
Hummingbirds	77
Thunder	78
Rinse and Repeat	79
September 2010	80
Tradition	81
Wallpaper and Cranes	82
Sepulchers	83
The New Owners	84
Passage	85
Garrison Keillor Reminds Me This Morning	86
What We Keep	88
Palimpsest	90
It's a Lonely Day	92
Cycle	93

Flowers grow in mud,

but open petal by petal,
fragrant.

Birds sing in cages,
fly when freed.

Forest, Garden, Sea

Dark Forests and Mountain Tops

I have lit a lantern
and forded streams,
turned over rocks
as adept as any bear
foraging for ants
upon which to feed.
I have built carefully
controlled campfires
breathing in breezes
wafting with wooden
kindling, cooking
creatures with crackling
succulent skin.
I am a survivor.
What's more,
I can lead anyone
willing to take the trip
along the same deep,
dark path as ably as any sherpa
climbing Mt. Everest
where air thins,
stomachs empty,
heads pound.

Inside us all dwell
forest creatures
set there without
ill intent. The forest
is only dark at its depth.
The edges let in light,
and as one climbs
higher altitudes
dark forests fade.

Thinning air forces
gasping which is where
the heart pumps strongest.

The Hawk: Part One

It struck with a thud,
but did not break the glass.
The oily sheen from its plumage
left an impression on the pane
that would remain months,
and a red shoulder feather
rested in the grass.
It must have been hunting
another rabbit. Their entry
and egress point was a few feet
below that window,
and perhaps a foot
from the edge of the house
where the fence gate post
stood sentinel, guarding the yard
and garden from rabbits.
The tercel cleared the backyard
throughout the summer—
frustrating our coonhound
that loved sniffing out rabbit trails
first thing in the morning
before relieving himself
and wanting breakfast.
Bones collected
below the nest high
in the hackberry tree
along the edge of the yard.
They bleached white in the sun
stripped clean of meat,
tendons, and marrow.
And strips of fur collected
amid heuchera, hostas,
irises, and roses.

Rabbits persisted besting the hawk
by escaping through that dug out spot,
hiding between the house
and the hose reel box
until they could escape
into the shrubbery thorns
and shelter below the dwarf spruce
until the last one fed the hen and eyas.

The Hawk: Part Two

The sun blots his shape to a silhouette
as he climbs the hackberry,
stopping to secure himself
and throw his rope yet higher
to another branch
to support his weight
and the chain saw
dangling from his left hip.
The broken branch
threatens the neighbor's property.
Other branches weigh down
a substantial limb likely to fall
when ice crystals create lacy layers
on which snow will stick
when winter arrives.
As the climber saws,
a nest is exposed
in which our predator birds
resided all summer.
The tercel and hen
raised eyas they hoped
would join the hunting kettle.
As the climber ascends,
the red-shouldered hawk circles.

Winging Home

Above the cloud cover,
below the March moon
with the North Star
guiding them,
a Canada Goose
wings north heading home
honking a formation change
for the flock.

I envy their detachment
from the gravity of Earth
holding me in place
as I miss housewarmings,
two birthdays,
a christening, funerals,
sick grandchildren,
an ailing daughter,
but a vaccination
signals a course change
magnetic north

taking me home.

The Forest

A robin rises to a branch
with moss to line a nest
in which to lay blue eggs.

A black bear paws
and maws ants from a log,
then seeks another.

Saplings twist toward
sunlight reaching through
shadows of aging ancestors.

A man wanders a path—
hat in hand—and greets a woman
strolling past a prowling fox

and a rabbit as still as a statue
amid sounds of sough
is saved by the strollers.

Northwestern Wilds

Few had seen such a sight.
And townspeople wanted the meat
for their sled dogs when they heard
that two moose died in battle over a female
near Unalakleet, in northwest Alaska.
Antlers locked like dove-tailed joints,
from the frozen water dusted
with fresh snow like powdered sugar
on a Monte Cristo.

One giant had pierced the other's skull—
both drowned when they fell into the stream.
A taxidermist used a pick and chain saw
to free the ice from their necks,
then cut off their heads
for an unusual wall mount.

Mutual Trust

In a market parking lot, a man
returns to his cab—arms
filled with supplies he intends to take to shelter,

or perhaps to flee with ahead
of the increasing threat as winds
whip harder, and rain thrusts from vertical

to horizontal. He unloads his purchases,
then remembers the passenger window
is open, toggles it closed,

watches glass rise, and stares deep
into yellow eyes. A hawk
with a brown-speckled broken wing

rests on gray upholstery.
The cabby thinks a moment,
speaks kindly to this fare, suggesting

he move on. The bird remains risking man
over nature. The cabby exits to the market
and returns with butcher paper

filled with reddish-gray chicken hearts
and feeds a grateful refugee,
whom he names, *Harvey.*

Otis

He pads along the edge of the road
wet with early rain. His reddish fur
sheds moisture for now

as he takes his cues from humans
gathering supplies to ride out
the storm. He is known to residents

who are easy touches for brown eyes
that implore a snack here and there
along his daily path. No hand is available

for treats this day, so Otis helps himself
to a bag of dog chow perched low
on a shelf. Jaw, neck and withers strain

as his paws scratch along the tar,
sinking in rising water heading home
to shelter under a roof that houses

a dry cushion and a dish in need of kibble.

White Hair and Red Yarn

Down the road, in the brunt of the storm
and rising waters, elderly women bob
in the assisted living activities room

awaiting rescue as they wade with walkers
through waist-high water, schooling in submerged
wheelchairs, working crossword puzzles

and knitting red yarn into warm sweaters.

I Walk the Dog

It is early about six-thirty.
The pup is agitated,
but I convince him
to continue.
He's looking for something.
A coonhound, tracking
comes natural to him,
but this is different.
There's a bit of paranoia
I detect as we wind up the hill
and round the corner.
He wants to return home.
We're halfway on the one-mile walk
and I'd rather go forward.
A quarter mile later,
he calms a bit.
It's my turn to grow fearful.
Across the street—
about three lot-lengths ahead—
I see two large canines
loping like wolves.
The sun is rising
as they are swallowed
into the underbrush.
I pick up the pace,
and by now the dog
willingly heads home with me.

This Natural World

into which we moved
six years ago
from the Upper Midwest
to the middle climes
feels closer to a snowbird's dream.
We open the back door
and stroll, or work
the yard and gardens,
fresh, green,
near the city limits.
Fur and feather abound
with occasional reptiles,
but no fins from the pond
a block down the street—
yet.
There was once a strange
arrival and departure
of a crayfish on the sidewalk.
A red-shouldered hawk
may have dropped it
on the way to its nest
where it would dine al fresco,
or feed fledglings.
Every day is a new wonder.

Battlefields to Greenhouses

*Mathew Brady photographed the Civil War
hiring help to develop and print.*

Brady had a studied eye for subject matter,
depth of field, sharp focus, composition,
and emotion, we all learned.
I knew him first by his reputation,
for the fact that his photographs won awards.

So as war loomed, Mr. Brady
photographed the young idealistic
Unionist lads of the North
for what was—for many—their
last living portrait.

He told Mr. Lincoln,
that a spirit in his feet
told him to go, and he
received permission
to chronicle the war.

Shutter speeds—being what they were—
and war—being what it was—
turned Brady's eye to the aftermath of battles—
gruesome as they were—
and he left the depictions of battles themselves
to the canvas painters.

He failed his mission in many ways,
for he did not document locations, dates,
or credit the images' creators.
You see, he hired some men—
his own army of sorts—and equipped them
with traveling darkrooms.

Brady put together an exhibition
in D.C. that brought Antietam home:
their corpses told the story.
Americans saw the price of war—
one they thought would be brief.
And so, people did what comes natural:
they did not want to dwell
on the horror or the truth.

In the end, the government did not buy
these inspired visual poems
seen through a camera lens,
and scribed on albumin paper
from glass plates. They told the story—
like any good poetry—
through the use of the seen
and the unseen:
in the white spaces.

These were sadly beautiful,
and Brady was bankrupted, so I
did what I could to help him
out of his fix and feed his family.
I bought some of those glass plates.
He practically gave them away.
Money is money, food is food,
and charity is good for the soul.

The plates became my greenhouse panes
that trapped moisture that ran like tears
on droplets of capillary action down the dead
Unionists and Confederate images onto plants
below in this their second deaths.
Instead of feeding fields of wildflowers from below,
they watered cultivated flowers from above.

They watered white anemones like the pure spirits
of the dead. They watered irises—straight and tall,
heads fallen open flanked with bayonet leaves:
these fleur-de-lys. They watered platoons of orchids
too frail to support themselves without wood—
my personal army, I guess. And the sun
bleached their images—those plates that held their souls—
to ghostly faintness until they disappeared.

Splitting Hares

I sprinkle blood
around the gate
into the back garden.
I cannot help but feel I
lack the secret incantation
that will do the job.
This is not the first
attempt to outsmart
a persistent rabbit
bent on digging up
the yard. I've boarded
the bottom of the fence,
placed flagstone
and river rock in holes
paws have dug under gates,
and run water down
a grass covered warren.
I've sprayed plants
with unpleasant flavors,
and chased this bunny
up to twenty minutes
around the yard
hoping it would exit,
and I could plug that spot,
too. At last, coyote scent
stops this dance of futility,

for two days.

Protecting the Dray

The nest is damaged
and she takes on the home repair
with the dray inside.
A hole opens in the bottom
and three chirping red squirrels
spill out twelve feet up in branches.
Plop, plop, plop!

Fearing our adventurous pup,
she grabs one kit
by the scruff of its neck,
scanning the fence
for an exit. Finding one,
she flattens her body
and pushes the baby under
returning to the roots
of the maple tree
where another—
unschooled in climbing trunks—
scurries around in circles.
This one is larger
and she struggles to save it.

She scrambles within a foot
of our living room window
where the dog watches
in agitation as she—
in equal agitation—
searches for—and finds—her third baby.

The panic in her movements
turns my thoughts to this morning:
my daughter's difficult pregnancy.
She texted a sonogram
of our fourth grandson
who will spill from her womb
soon with the hope of a soft landing
in the face of danger.

Red Poppies

You told me
about the pistol,
and the shot gun
you kept at hand.
You told me
about the neighbor
who fed deer.
You told me
about the deer
that ate your flowers.
You told me
about previous disputes
with the neighbor.
You told me
he threatened harm
by poking his drunken,
bony, old finger
into your husband's
paunchy belly.
I have guns.
Ain't afraid to use 'em.
Ain't afraid to kill a man neither.
You told me
his words delivered
in a drunken slur,
on a hot day,
sent icy chills
through you.
So when I heard
about another neighbor
in yet another state
shot to death
by another husband
of another woman

—forgive me—
I thought of you.
I pictured
a shotgun
firing snake shot
like a Tarantino scene
with blood splatter
dotting your yard
like a field
of red poppies.

Mystery

The trowel plunges into soil,
striking a hard mass.
The gardener stops to work
the earth with gloved hands
clearing away loam that will support
spring bulbs near the lilies
in that garden plot.
Pulling tangles of creeping jenny
aside and lifting hosta leaves,
edges of engraved granite
speak to her in Spanish:
Established April 15.
But when? A section is scratched away
keeping this secret as well as the question
as to what exactly here was settled.

In the Wings

Caterpillars gathered
from milkweed fronds
in an empty lot
at the end of the block,
are carefully placed in
glass Mason jars with lids
pierced by nails and hammer
to prevent suffocation.

Milkweed stalks broken
between thumb
and index finger
ooze thick, sticky, prized
nectar for caterpillars
with groping mouths
that fill their gullets before
encasing themselves
hanging
upside-down from
jade chrysalides
on a diagonal expanse
of twig placed
just so.

Eight lots south
of our house
was home for jumping
and flying, green grasshoppers,
crawling worms that inched
up hairy stalks to feed
and to become food
for scrounging birds
with hunting beaks:

a moving microcosm
of Nature's cycles advancing
in near silence, but for
thick-throated chirps
burst like
gaseous burps
released after a
satiating meal.

Hummingbirds Hover Out My Office Window

The green one floats on air
as though on a string
above a crib to entertain
and for which to reach out.
It sups from the knock-out roses
reminding me I ought to prune them
for longer blooming
and more wings
a-flutter.
Months of isolation make me
envious of the ease with which this bird
interacts with the world
and its kind.

Fate

The snake rests in the path of her truck
which she wants to back out
under the overhead door.
It stretches out as thick as her thin wrist
which supports the garden hose
she uncoils toward the sunning creature.
The water is icy, and its flow freezes
the cold-blooded reptile in place.
The woman grabs a shovel—
long-handled—from the display
on the garage wall and—with caution—
she scoops up this napper,
transports it to wooded yard
behind the garage.
She flings the snake
deep into the woods
where it catches high in a tree.
It hangs there (still semi-coiled)
the color of the aspen branch
from which it will warm
its cold body,
and determine
its own fate.

Shoebox

A robin strikes the window
breaking its neck, but is still
alive trying to right itself.
I am near the glass,
empty a shoebox
of baseball cards,
and grab Kleenex
for a cushion.
I slide the door open in its track,
and in the red salvia
I see two yellow eyes
intent on the bird.
Away runs the cat
as I lift the lifeless avian,
feathers as bent as its neck
and place it
in the cardboard coffin.

Roadkill

Ahead in the road,
in a small dip
at the bottom of a hill,
I see fresh roadkill.
It isn't yet flattened
and unrecognizable.
I calculate the incline
ahead, the speed limit,
and decide to straddle it,
avoiding fender damage—
should a car crest the hill—
or fresh blood
in my wheel wells.
I realize as I have considered—
rather coldly—my
inconvenience and distaste,
it has heard my engine
approaching and tried
to right itself.
It's a baby squirrel:
back broken, tail twitching,
front legs clawing air,
gaining no traction,
and I have no time
to change course
to end its pain.

Composting Irises

I always thought they were Mother's irises,
when they were Father's—for her.
She raised the family;
he raised flowers.
And so, it was with my parents.

Father suffered from PTSD—
before it was an acronym—
after the war. He wasn't treated.
Mother bore the bruises,
but never gave up on the love.

She missed him terribly when he died.
His pillowcase remained unwashed
for five years until she followed him
in the last days of her journey
confident she would either see him again,
or rest in peace.

Covering the last raw space
amid the irises,
I shovel one more spadeful.

Caterpillar

The chenille covers
in the garage
for the flowerbeds
were off limits
to we children,
but when a playmate
appeared with whom
to transform into a superhero
the blankets made perfect capes.
Chenille is French for caterpillar
and made the change poignant—
lacking either a chrysalis
or a phone booth.

My superpower was invisibility
to Mother's eye as I sneaked past her
for Band-Aids when I cut my leg
down to the bone in the garage
on my Schwinn Tornado fender.

Beneath Missouri's Bootheel

miles add up behind us,
and those ahead shrink
as we travel the dark road.

Along a stretch of highway,
west of the Mississippi
are fields of cotton bolls

open like popped corn.
The sky is a gray November
haze of rain that mutes colors

like that of an Impressionist's subject
seen through gentle tears.
Fields of long, low expanses

of plants are punctuated
by an occasional corn stalk
that survived rotational farming.

Some stand tall. Some stoop
as though they are picking cotton.
Along the road's shoulder grow

communities of sumac. It's late fall
and many branches are bare:
soaked dark from precipitation

exposing arms and fingers of wood
raised as if in supplication
topped with seed pods swollen

like sore fingers after harvesting
by hand. Thinning fronds hang
below these prayerful plants

dripping heavy mist like blood.
White lint remnants from a nearby
harvest have settled atop.

Beneficiaries

I wish to leave the iris rhizomes
and daylily tubers for my daughters.
They connect three generations.
They belonged to their grandmothers
and now to their mother.
In protecting them from the truth
about their father,
we lost the closeness
that still lives in my heart and memory.
Flowers are sent to the sick and dying.
This seems appropriate.

Aesop's Fable: Reward

The first time I met the reptile,
it was still as a stick,
a long broom,
black and stretched its full length
on the edge of the budding blades
of grass along the scar
from the new yard drain.
I bent to pick up the debris
soon realizing it was alive.
I caught the coonhound
and put him in the house
before he knew it was there
letting the serpent
live another day.

The next time felt like an Aesop's fable:
reward for a past mercy.
It writhed in the grass
in what looked like pain,
but it was constricting breath
from a mole burrowing
through the backyard—
nature's garden tool.
The snake's head was exposed
and pulled back with each
muscle contraction
as its slick rope body
tightened underneath the turf.

Another Day

A turtle near the heuchera
periscopes its head
swiveling left then right
assessing the best maneuvers
to make, avoiding danger—
a captain avoiding torpedoes.

Hearing the mower as my husband
powers it up to level stragglers
from yesterday's mow,
I exit the gate to retrieve a shovel
since the turtle hissed at me,
making itself appear fearsome—
it worked.

By the time I return—
one minute perhaps—
I find him over twenty feet
from where I had left him.
He had climbed over a brick
into the garden
and was nearing a sculpted turtle.

Feeling like a savior,
I scoop it up in the metal
and find a depression under the fence
where I deposit it to live another day.

Medusa of the Deep

A bloom floats like a dream
along shallow, warm,
salt-water coast. Like a desert
after crashing thunder
follows bright flashes
amid downpours that fill salt pans
that bloom with magical, delicate petals
from Mighty slight-of-hand.

This bloom of jellyfish
feeds on plankton warmed by radiation
nearly ninety-three million miles
above. These floating sea belles
complete with tentacle clappers,
transparent to predators,
stuffed with mesoglea
like truffle's cream-filling,
with stings as fatal to man
as any femme fatale, live
briefly, beautifully, colorfully.

Gliding and self-propelling
powerfully along ocean currents,
stinging prey with venom
that paralyses like Medusa's face
was believed to have turned men
to stone.

Waddles

In the water,
they are called a *raft*.
On land they are *waddles*.
Emperor penguins—
by whatever they are called—
share parenting in the wild.

They travel long distances
to begin families in harsh,
craggy outcrops along coastal
waters that crash cold waves,
and where predators are plenty.

They take turns warming eggs
until wet hatchlings break
through shells,
then dry to downy feathers
reminiscent of stuffed toys
washed then dried on air-fluff.
They are loved.
They are protected.
They are hungry.

In this parental relationship,
mother brings home the bacon,
trekking far expanses, feeding upon
what will be regurgitated to the young,
while father stays home
with the young tucked
beneath him as he stands sentinel.

Onsra

In memory of Phil:
Onsra *means to love for the last time.*

I dreamt I was a nautilus spiral
with iridescent interior,
amid silt in ocean depths
unnoticed,
but visible
to those willing to see me.
I felt warm waves
caress me as if an infant
bathed in amniotic fluids
beneath mother's beating heart.
My gaze rose to the surface waters
where light filtered through green
gauzy floating plankton. Bodies
moved dreamily,
slowly rocking,
cradling an infant
about to drift to sleep.

Then I realized
family surrounded a young man
buoying him up, baptizing him
with waves of love.
Soft words, low tones
crooned soothingly of his love
of water: to be near it, on it, in it,
to feel it purify, quench, renew.
Like pallbearers,
they surrounded him.
They became his eyes,
his ears, his lips,
his limbs by which to move about,

and to embrace as each
learned to love for the last time
from amniotic womb
to saving pools
beyond the veil.

Accidental Fishing

An accident ahead in the road
slows traffic in the heavy mist.
We stop the car waiting
for the wrecker to clear a lane.
With nothing to do but wait,
I watch pools of water eddy
around small piles of pebbles
and the colors of raised oils
from the light rain on our pitted path.

In my mind the colors shift and swirl,
like rainbow sheen
that deepens with each tug
to start a choked outboard motor.
Then the boat speeds along to a secret
fishing spot on Platte Lake.
The sun burns my cheeks.
The wind knots my hair.
I reel in fish in a tug-o-war,
and they ballet in the boat bottom
as luminescent scales
flash under Minnesota's summer sun.

Brackish-water Crab

There is a type of crab
that lives in brackish water
along intertidal mud flats,
lagoons, and swamps,
that made me think of you today
as I read with interest
of its inability to exist
in either fresh or salt water
for any extended time.

The males have one claw
that is out of balance
and much larger than the other
and can be regrown if damaged or lost.
It lives in hardened shells,
eats sediment,
and engages in senseless combat
for female attention.

Bullhead

She slides her left gloved hand
down the length of its thick body
encasing the spiny stingers
as she pulls the swallowed hook
with a long-handled pliers
from deep inside the stomach.
Red stringy blobs of offal
hang from the hook—
the worm is still attached.
She smashes its head
on the dock and tosses it
to the sandy beach
out of the reach
of foamy waves.
She repeats this ritual
whenever she catches a bullhead.
She knows how to protect herself.

An Artistic Interlude

An Orchestra

once moved through me.
At the crescendo
the kettledrum
lifted me out of my seat
to my feet as if on a string.

In a moment of deep despair,
the final blessing at mass
moved through me
in the same way—
as if a woodwind section
summoned me, drove me
like autumn leaves
before a wind.

Period Piece

After Frederick James's
Twilight on Quality Hill, Kansas City, 1946

The Victorian era home—
under a hipped roof—
stands static in time,
but for one second-floor window
where a curtain
appears to breathe out
like an escaping spirit.
Outside, the contemporary
world trundles past
lighting the shadows
to something discernible
as they crowd wet evening streets
with the forward movement
of Hudsons,
Packards,
Saratogas—
even the Red Wing
truck has wings!
A man canes the stairs
of the colonnaded
portico out of rain's
reach with one hand
holding up the past—
a Herculean task.
The only hint of movement
in his life is the white flag
of a realty sign
planted in the fading grass.
Denuded trees flank the building
in this fall season of his life.
Above, an airplane leaves the house
behind as it heads along the continuum
of time and of space.

Journey

*The journey of one thousand miles
begins with one step.*
                           —Lao Tzu

Though one's voice
is but a chime
of hollowed wood
waving in the wind
like spirits of the dead
moving faintly
between this world
and the next,
speaking one's truth—
however molecular
it may be to others—
is the first step
in the journey
to fulfillment.

River Bank, 1910

After Daniel Garber's River Bank, 1910

No bathing beauty
or contemplative beau
along the river's edge:
only gravel
and sand.
No sweep of fall leaves,
or peaceful snow feathers
covering branches.

An *en plein air* of colors
soft, sunlit air
thick with summer heat
resting on lazy water
along muddy bank
where lush trees weep
graceful as Degas' ballerinas.

Driftwood settles giving shelter
to forest denizens and supports vines
of red berries for scavengers—
human and not.

Form and Function

At the art gallery,
I ponder a creation
of hand-woven,
hammered copper,
dapped in colorful enamels
of natural shades—
a stiff weave of metal
hammered porous
as nest or broken egg.

At home,
outside my kitchen window,
a red-breasted robin
weaves twigs, spent stems,
stalks, roots and mud
with beak, bottom, breast.
An act of instinct
nestled in an open,
wooden box
hanging on a fence
in my new garden.
She abandons hope
of hatching a brood
here this year:
too active, noisy,
while fruits and vegetables
nest in an open colander
near my sink.

Fractured Since 1848

Texas was annexed from Mexico in 1845
sparking the Mexican War ending in 1848.
After Duilio Barnabe's La Serveuse, circa 1959–1961.

We stand in light
making beds,
washing laundry,
kissing your children
good night
before we walk home
to our children.

In full sun, we are but brown
shadows, clouded by your eyes
as we pick your harvest.

Our ancestors owned
and worked this land
before you moved the borders.

We stand before you
fractured in shadow
and in light.

Anita, Christine and E. Jean

> *An homage to* Abraham, Martin and John,
> *by Richard Louis Haller*

Has anybody here seen our old friend Anita Hill?
Can you tell me what we've lost?
She warned a lot of people, but no one would hear.
The first chink in justice appeared.

Has anybody here seen our old friend Christine Blasey Ford?
Can you tell me what we've lost?
She warned a lot of people, but no one would hear.
Autonomy has disappeared.

Has anybody here seen our old friend E. Jean Carroll?
Can you tell me what we've lost?
She lost her voice, now it has reappeared.
Face your rapists while they are here.

Didn't they love the freedoms that we've all lost?
Didn't they try to keep good things for you and me,
so we'd stay free?
Yet someday soon, our vote may fall in ruin.

Has anybody here been dragged through the mud?
Can you tell me what you've lost?
Let's fight the fight, as we walk up that hill
with Anita, Christine and E. Jean Carroll.

Beloveds and Others

Cafuné

is the Portuguese word
for becoming tangled
in a lover's hair.
That very action
may also disentangle
silky strands of feeling
beyond that comforting tickle.
It creates a cocoon
that says:
become something new,
and beautiful with me.

Gardening

The absence of your love
once filled the bed nightly
as you lay near me.
That changed with divorce.
Your absence gave way
for space to be filled
with the presence of a man
who knows love is fragile,
and requires planting,
watering,
pruning,
not simply fertilizing.

Cleaning Fish

The filet knife
cuts the length
of the sunfish's belly
filled with worms.
Dad's fingers
tease out the stringy red
rubber-band guts.
A roundish red blob
once pumped blood,
but now lays in a pile
of offal from crappies
and sunnies
alike: internal detritus.
Metallic scales
piled like fallen snow.
Eyes blank, staring orbs
like cataracts
that restrained luster
from Grandpa's solemn face.

Strategies

I play the Queen of Hearts
on the King of Spades
hoping to free up the Diamond
Ace and start building bottom to top.
As I gaze at the possibilities
in front of me to win at solitaire,
I listen to the comforting hum
of the dishwasher scrubbing residue.
I think of my childhood kitchen
in my leisure after dinner.
My parents cozy on the sofa
together listening to the war coverage
holding on to hope my brothers
will receive *4F* status. My sister
purges dinner into the toilet,
then primps her hair before her date.
One brother watches The Twilight Zone,
two play softball with neighborhood boys
in good health awaiting their fates
with low Selective Service lottery numbers.

Friday Afternoons

Mother often laughed
when her hairdresser
stood behind her
at our kitchen table
arranging her hair
and spraying it
while smoking—
flicking ashes into a shot glass
between her voluptuous breasts—
talking at a speed
difficult to understand,
which was probably best.
Mother said she was *colorful;*
I called her *educational.*

Before Sunrise

Father had been dead
for five years when Mother
spoke about my ill health
as an infant.
I was hospitalized—
first for dehydration
brought on by

digestive upsets,
then with shingles—
before my first birthday.
This is how we knew
I had prenatal chicken pox.
She told me that my father
comforted me in the late hours
of the night, consoling me as I
cried in pain.

Now I often wonder
if those dark hours
before sunrise solidified
our relationship.

It's the Feast of St. Nicholas Again

and fourteen-years
have passed since Father died:
no coins,
no fruit,
no small gifts,
nor toys
in my shoe—
yet, memories
sweet as Christmas oranges,
more fun than finger puppets,
these coins of wealth
fill my mind—
small gifts for my heart.

The Kiss

Their relationship
often had rocks in the road,
but there were never speed bumps.
I must have been invisible
for a moment as I watched
them embrace and kiss.
It wasn't their date night
in which they dressed up,
went out for a juicy prime rib
for Mother and frog legs for Father,
then hit the dance floor
like Fred and Ginger.
Father led. Mother followed.
It was impossible to recreate in my life—
though I tried.

Rearview Mirror

Certainly, the impact killed the dog.
I was too young to understand
obvious damage the owners saw.
I was at a distance.
Our station wagon
was going one way
and the oncoming car another.
It swerved well before necessary
and the dog darted in the way
as it changed focus from one master
to the other.
A twist of fate.
Though sometimes I think
about that moment in my childhood,
it is partly the coldness
with which those walkers responded
that stays with me.
They kept walking.
No flinching.
No examination of the animal.
No loving response.
The man simply scooped up their pet
by a limp leg never breaking stride
and lobbed it off the road
into the tall grasses.
I can still see my father's eyes
look at me in the rearview mirror
hoping I had not seen it.

Hummingbirds

On the dusty windowsill,
early evening sunlight
deepens the pastel colors
painted on porcelain pinions
spread open in flight. Father
collected figurines
of finely featured hummingbirds.
He hung red sugary feeders
near a window in his summer home
where tiny flitting birds
fed with quick movements
in and out to sip, maneuvering
with the skill of dogfighters.
It seemed so effortless to his eye
as wings beat too rapidly to detect.
When nesting began, father
watched as the females
employed beaks, chests and rumps
pushing moss, lichen, twigs,
leaves, even dryer lint
into demitasse shape with spider's
sticky webbing. They built them
camouflaged in high altitudes
as snug as his tail gunner
seat in the B-17 that carried him
humming high above Europe
to bomb bridges,
ammunition dumps,
railroads, and battlefields.
Did he think of the parachute silk
strapped to his back
as wings to escape when bombs
burst the fuselage?

Thunder

A flash of light brightens the room
through the rattan blinds
that flank the headboard
of the darkened bedroom.

A distant, low rumble begins
like the sound of resin balls
that will crash and tumble pins
scattering them where they
will be fed into a gathering arm
at the end of polished alleys.

Dad bowled on Wednesday nights
for years. He was good. One night
he bowled a near perfect 300 game.
His picture was in the Minneapolis
Star and Tribune. He clipped the article
and kept it for years in an envelope.

When he died, Mom became its keeper
along with other detritus of his life
all neatly organized in a bureau drawer.
He was proud of that accomplishment—
this from a WWII vet who served
in the European Theatre earning
a Purple Heart still in its box
resting next to that envelope.

Rinse and Repeat

I watch the water
stream from the faucet
and swirl down the drain
counterclockwise.
My fingers remove toothpaste
that has marred the porcelain
pushing it down toward
the miniature cyclone
I have created.
I wet my finger
rubbing out the residue,
then rinse my hands.
I am sad as I recall
Dad's frustration with my hesitation
to do the very same
more than fifty years ago.
He disliked a dirty sink.
I let him down then,
but not now.
I don't want to wash
his memory down the drain
like the Coriolis effect,
so I squeeze toothpaste
into the basin,
and rinse and repeat.

September 2010

Mother died on
Labor Day weekend.
The statement might seem random,
but Mother was preparing me
for the end—which she knew was near.
She had warned me
about things I would see,
remaining a mother to the end.

Some I knew.
Some were outlined
in the Hospice manual—
a guide to loss.
We shared signals
she was unaware
she was showing,
but she knew what they meant
and was happy to have
someone who was not
afraid to acknowledge
her time was limited.

Tradition

Her hands touch the smooth skin
and gently squeeze the fruit
twisting it slightly on the branch
testing its ripeness for jelly.
Grandma places some in her apron
and disappears to the kitchen.
The fruit I pick is firm, sour
and is wrenched from the branch
under the afternoon sun.

That was then.
This is now.
I see her hands on her chest.
Black rosary woven through her fingers.
Hair tidy.
Navy blue dress.
Perhaps her only dress.

All this from the receipts
tucked in a drawer Mother
kept from the arrangements
over forty years ago.

Wallpaper and Cranes

She wallpapered over the truth,
but it changed nothing,
so she peeled back the edges
to find the home that was once
a home of lightness
was now one of darkness
where grief, denial, anger,
bargaining, depression,
moved on to blessed acceptance
when she took flight
like origami cranes
that bring success,
good fortune
and the heart's desire.

Now she stands
next to her garden companion—
a sculpted crane—
hip deep in purple irises
burgeoning with blooms
of wisdom and yellow day lilies
in waiting like a mother's
sacrifices for her children.

Sepulchers

We step into the exhibit—
a cavernous, dimly lit room
with sporadic lights like eyes
of gods watching from above
over these petrified corpses
that occupy room
after room with bodies
mummified to eternity.

Desert climate and peat
bogs unintentionally
preserved bones, hair, teeth,
nails, and internal organs of some.
Others have undergone elaborate
processes with desiccants.

Here, there is a reverence
both expected from patrons
and demanded by humanity
for those lying in state now
in hand-hewed sarcophagi
that tell their tales
on display under glass.

And now, as I stand in this dark,
vast space under the watchful eyes
of the exhibit lights, I consider
how timeless the need is to preserve
our stories.

The New Owners

removed the currant shrub
with red berries,
so it is no longer outside
Mom and Dad's east-facing bedroom window
where I peered between Venetian blinds
watching migrating cedar wax wings
strip the fruit every year as I grew.

Now neither they nor I can return
along our life migrations.

Passage

Once a bulb
planted in the garden
of my womb,
you emerged gangly and wet,
but stalked out lovely
as a calla lily
that occasionally shows blossoms,
but still withholds that splash of color
until the next cycle
of life—the next passage.
As years faded
you grew taller,
stronger,
more colorful,
and you showed impressively
in the larger garden.

Now you have graduated
and will no longer be fenced in,
no longer walk the line,
but cross it,
like a goddess sheds restrictions,
grows in virtue,
love,
fertility
and multiplies.

Garrison Keillor Reminds Me This Morning

that Mount St. Helens
erupted on this day in 1980—
the day my second daughter
returned home in my arms
from the hospital where she
erupted from my womb
two days earlier
essentially dead,
like many who
died in that cataclysm.

Pelting glacial ice
and debris rose to eighty feet
collapsing the north face
with mud spreading
fifty miles. Fifty-seven people
died and thousands of animals.
Ash cluttered the atmosphere
as far as Wisconsin
where we lived.

And so began our lives
together with my miniature
Mount St. Helens.
After slipping from my south face,
blue with her life cord
tight around her neck
and into the hands of the doctor,
she was too quiet.
Too disengaged.
Then she pushed away
like that mud, stone and ice,
breathing our shared atmosphere.

What We Keep

My family has a history of
early Alzheimer's. I have
held onto so very many things
throughout the years to
preserve memories like
strawberry jam, or perhaps
like sauerkraut.

This recent purge
includes a red, white,
and blue basketball.
At first, I was hurt
that it was a *women's*
ball, but it was a good fit
for me and I spent many hours
wearing the nubs off from
contact with the asphalt,
and the backboard.

As my girls grew,
they stopped playing
with me. A family
moved in next door
to our home.

Their teen-aged son
was disabled from
a fiery school bus
and semi-truck collision.
He carried with him
many physical handicaps,
but the one that was the
most difficult for him
was his inability
to communicate clearly.

Either his speech improved
from our conversations,
or my listening improved from
our conversations. Either way,
he began talking.
We shot basketball from
various spots on the driveway
over and over again.

As time went by,
I would hear his teasing
taunt from the dining room
window twenty feet from
the hoop, "Aiiiirr baaallll!"

Palimpsest

After the divorce,
a woman asked
if I enjoyed rewriting my life.
I answered,
I am unearthing it.
You see . . .

Indiana Jones taught students
that archeology
is mainly research
and an open mind. Know history,
and geography
before shoveling the excavation site.
Trench the location
and mark it with yellow tape
that lets the locals
know not to cross the line
as important work
is in the troweling
beyond. It is often sacred ground,
and ought to be treated with respect
as hands fill buckets and trugs
using hand pickaxes,
or spatulas with educated patience
before covering the site
with protective tarpaulins
at day's end. The work itself
is dangerous, and the deeper the dig,
the more need for helmet
and safety glasses,
for one encounters archeological
surprises along the way.

First aid kits
are a must, for even gloves
often cannot protect the digger
from shards of broken pottery
that once held the liquids
that sustained and entertained populations.
After picks have cleared an area
down to its depths where foundations
emerge, sieves and brushes
set to work with delicate strokes
discovering how a civilization
once lived in a populated area.
Most sites show levels of sophistication
from the arts, to the value of education,
to military defense, beyond the civil
engineering of the village. Bones
reveal the people's physical adaptations
to the environment, or what they
ate, what ate them, or even who they ate.

What is revealed in such tedious work
is the buried truth that lays to rest
the facts like forensics in a murder case.

It's a Lonely Day

to be outside
at a picnic table
waiting for my brother-in-law
to emerge from the clinic
where his eyes are examined
after cataract surgery.
With the pandemic,
my husband and I
are not allowed inside.
We sit shaded by an oak.
He reads a book,
I work a word-find puzzle.
A tiny reddish spider
walks across the page
like he is pointing
the obvious to me.
I watch his diagonal movement
as I circle another word
and keep him company.

Cycle

The sapling twists its branches
in spirals and right angles
or whatever convolution
it needs to find sunshine
to feed its chlorophyll
filled leaves uplifted
like supplicants' hands.
It grows in near shadow
under forest canopy, unaware
that its time will come
as mature trees give way
to heavy branches felled
by snow, relentless twisting
winds, boring bugs that bear blight,
or drought that dries deep roots.
The old will fall to the forest floor
feeding microbes that nourish soil
their offspring sup like milk
from mother's breast. Life
goes on, and the sapling
straightens, no longer seeking
sunshine that was always there,
but soaking up rays that will mature
them as they produce seeds to
start this process once more.

I remember the way you twisted yourself
to catch my eye while I cooked dinner.
You rushed in and asked questions
that required considered thought
never waiting to hear answers
before darting off and thinking
of new ways to ask the very
same things in very different ways.

And now, you have two small sons
of your own. I picture the process
repeating itself and smile
at the image of curiosity incarnate,
and I wish for you contentment.

About the Author

Nancy Jo Allen was born and raised in Minneapolis, Minnesota and moved to Wisconsin, where she spent thirty-four years owning and operating a few businesses of her own before closing one to work with her husband in another business as vice-president, production manager, and department head. In Eau Claire, Wisconsin, Allen earned a baccalaureate majoring in English Literature with a double minor in Creative Writing and Theatre. She was inducted as a member of Sigma Gamma Zeta II honor society in her undergraduate years.

Allen divorced in 2005 and was accepted to a graduate program through Spalding University in Louisville, Kentucky, where she earned a Master of Fine Arts of Writing degree with the emphasis on playwriting. She was a student editor for *The Louisville Review* and won first place in a Metroversity short fiction contest while attending the graduate program. Allen's graduate creative thesis was read by both the Actor's Theatre of Louisville and by the August Wilson and the Playwrights' Center in St. Paul, Minnesota.

She quit her job and sold her condominium to move to Minnesota, where she spent the last year of her mother's life with her while working with senior services. After her mother's death, Allen enrolled into a program that earned her an Associates of Applied Science degree, allowing her to be a certified and licensed practitioner working as an Occupational Therapy Assistant (COTA/L) in a variety of allied health facilities.

She began writing poetry in the fall of 2013. Allen married again in 2016, and she and her husband have published several collections of poetry separately since then. Allen's photographs, short stories, and fiction have been published in a variety of journals both nationally and internationally. Her first poetry collection *Wrinkles in Time and in Love* (2021) is available through Kelsay Books and Amazon. Allen currently lives in Columbia, Missouri with her husband Terry and their dog Jayden. She is the mother of two daughters and the grandmother of four boys.

www.ingramcontent.com/pod-product-compliance
Lightning Source LLC
Chambersburg PA
CBHW031200160426
43193CB00008B/456